The
Neighborhood
MOTHER
GOOSE

For August

# The Neighborhood MOTHER GOOSE

## By Nina Crews

**Greenwillow Books**
*An Imprint of HarperCollins Publishers*
Amistad

# The Rhymes

Hey diddle diddle!
The cat and the fiddle,
The cow jumped
Over the moon.
The little dog laughed
To see such sport,
And the dish ran away
With the spoon.

7

Roses are red,
Violets are blue,
Sugar is sweet,
And so are you.

Dance, little baby, dance up high!
Never mind, baby, Mother is by.
Crow and caper, caper and crow,
There, little baby, there you go.
Up to the ceiling, down to the ground,
Backward and forward, round and round.
Dance, little baby, and Mother shall sing,
With the merry gay coral,
Ding, ding-a-ding, ding!

Pat-a-cake,
Pat-a-cake,
Baker's man.
Bake me a cake
As fast as you can.
Pat it, and prick it,
And mark it with B.
Put it in the oven
For baby and me.

Pease porridge hot,
Pease porridge cold,
Pease porridge in the pot,
Nine days old.
Some like it hot,
Some like it cold,
Some like it in the pot,
Nine days old.

Jack,
Be nimble,
Jack, be quick,
Jack, jump over the candlestick.

Cobbler, cobbler,
Mend my shoe.
Get it done by half past two.
Stitch it up, and stitch it down,
Make the finest shoes in town.

When I was a little boy,
I washed my mother's dishes.
I put my finger in my ear,
And pulled out
Little fishes.

My mother called me
Good boy,
And bid me
Pull out more.
I put my finger
In my ear, and
Pulled out
Fourscore.

Georgie Porgie,
Pudding and pie,
Kissed the girls
And made them cry.
When the boys
Came out to play,
Georgie Porgie
Ran away.

17

Pussy cat, pussy cat,
Where have you been?
I've been to London
To visit the queen.
Pussy cat, pussy cat,
What did you do there?
I frightened a little mouse
Under her chair.

19

To market,
To market,
To buy a fat pig.
Home again,
Home again,
Jiggety jig.
To market,
To market,
To buy a fat hog.
Home again,
Home again,
Jiggety jog.
To market,
To market,
To buy a plum bun.
Home again,
Home again,
Market is done.

Twinkle, twinkle,
Little star,
How I wonder what you are!
Up above the world so high,
Like a diamond in the sky.

As your bright and tiny spark
Lights the traveler in the dark,
Though I know not what you are,
Twinkle, twinkle,
Little star.

The itsy-bitsy spider
Climbed up the waterspout.
Down came the rain
And washed the spider out.
Out came the sunshine,
Dried up all the rain.
The itsy-bitsy spider
Climbed the spout again.

Little Miss Muffet
Sat on a tuffet,
Eating her curds and whey.
There came a big spider
Who sat down beside her
And frightened
Miss Muffet
Away.

25

There was a little girl
Who had a little *curl*
Right in the middle
Of her forehead.
When she was good,
She was very, very good,
But when she was bad,
She was horrid.

27

Ride a cockhorse to
Banbury Cross
To see a fine lady
Upon a white horse.

Rings on her fingers
And bells on her toes,
And she shall have music
Wherever she goes.

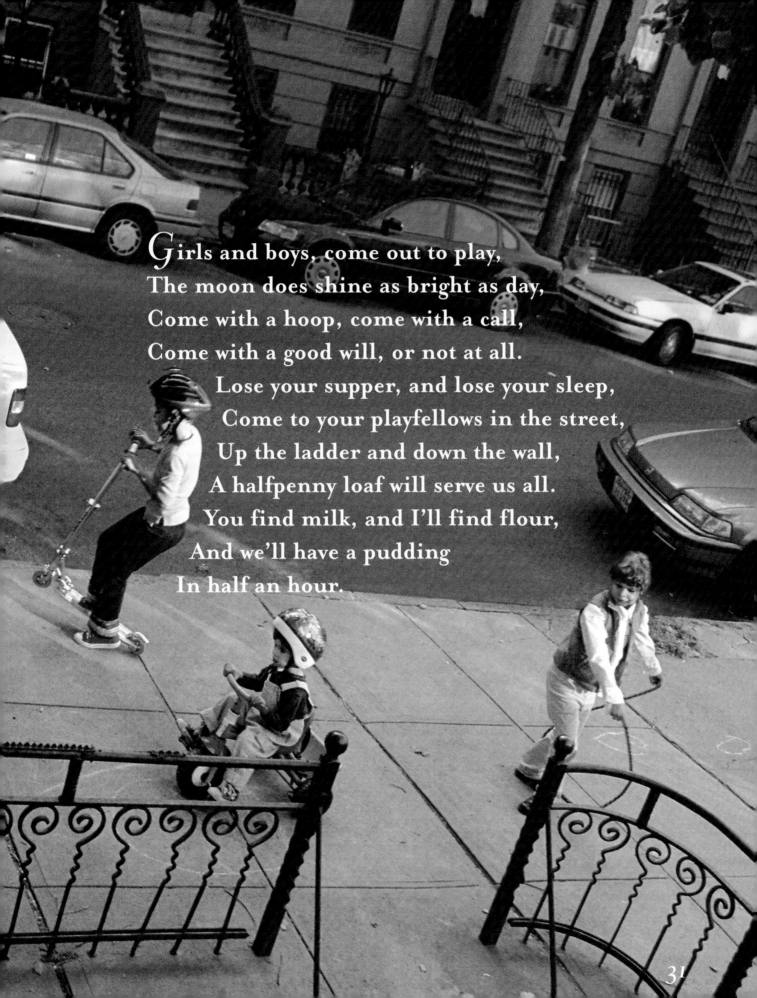

Girls and boys, come out to play,
The moon does shine as bright as day,
Come with a hoop, come with a call,
Come with a good will, or not at all.
Lose your supper, and lose your sleep,
Come to your playfellows in the street,
Up the ladder and down the wall,
A halfpenny loaf will serve us all.
You find milk, and I'll find flour,
And we'll have a pudding
In half an hour.

A was
An apple pie,
B bit it,
C cut it,

D dealt it,
E eat it,
F fought for it,
G got it,

H had it,
I inspected it,
J jumped for it,
K kept it,

L longed for it,
M mourned for it,
N nodded at it,
O opened it,

P peeped in it,
Q quartered it,
R ran for it,
S stole it,

T took it,
U upset it,
V viewed it,
W wanted it,

X, Y, Z,
And ampersand
All wished
For a piece
In hand.

33

*Humpty Dumpty*
Sat on a wall,
Humpty Dumpty
Had a great fall.
All the king's horses
And all the king's men
Couldn't put Humpty
Together again.

*Tweedledum* and *Tweedledee*
Agreed to have a battle,
For Tweedledum said Tweedledee
Had spoiled his nice new rattle.
Just then flew by a monstrous crow,
As big as a tar barrel,
Which frightened both the heroes so,
They quite forgot their quarrel.

36

*A*s I was going
Along, long, long,
A-singing a comical
Song, song, song,
The lane that I went was so
Long, long, long,
And the song
That I sung was as
Long, long, long,
And so I went
Singing
Along.

Mary, Mary, quite contrary,
How does your garden grow?
With silver bells and cockleshells
*And pretty maids all in a row.*

Touch blue,
Your wish will
Come true.

There was
An old woman
Tossed in a blanket,
Seventeen times as high as the moon,
But where she was going     no one could tell,
For under her arm she     carried a broom.
"Old woman, old woman, old woman," said I!
"Whither, ah, whither, ah, whither so high?"
"To sweep the cobwebs from the sky,
And I'll be with you
By and by."

Once I saw a little bird
Come hop, hop, hop;
And I cried, "Little bird,
Will you stop, stop, stop?"
I was going to the window
To say, How do you do?
But he shook his little tail,
And away he flew.

Jack and Jill
Went up the hill
To fetch a pail of water;
Jack fell down
And broke his crown,
And Jill came tumbling after.

There was an old woman
Who lived in a shoe.
She had so many children
She didn't know what to do.
She gave them some broth
Without any bread.
She scolded them soundly
And sent them
To bed.

45

Rain, rain, go away.
Come again another day;
*Little Johnny wants to play.*

Ring around the rosie,
A pocket full of posies;
*Ashes! Ashes!*
We all

fall

down.

*B*ow, *wow, wow.*
**Whose dog art thou?**
**Little Tom Tinker's dog.**
*Bow, wow, wow.*

One, two,
Whatever you do,
Start it well,
And carry it through.
Try, try, never say die.
Things will come right,
You know, by and by.

Lucy Locket
Lost her pocket.
Kitty Fisher found it.
Nothing in it,
Nothing in it,
But the binding
Round it.

51

Diddle diddle dumpling, my son John
Went to bed with his trousers on,
One shoe off, and one shoe on.
Diddle diddle dumpling, my son John.

Ladybug, Ladybug, fly away home!
Your house is on fire, your children all gone.
All but one, and her name is Ann,
And she crept under the pudding pan.

Hush-a-bye, baby,
On the treetop.
When the wind blows,
The cradle will rock.
When the bough breaks,
The cradle will fall.
Down will come baby,
Cradle and all.

The Man in the Moon
Looked out of the moon,
Looked out of the moon and said,
"'Tis time for all children on earth
To think about getting to bed!"

This little pig went to market.
This little pig stayed at home.
This little pig had roast beef.
This little pig had none.
And this little pig said,
"Wee, wee! I can't find my way home."

Peter Piper picked
A peck of pickled peppers;
A peck of pickled peppers
Peter Piper picked.

If Peter Piper picked
*A peck of pickled peppers,*
*Where's the peck of pickled peppers*
Peter Piper picked?

59

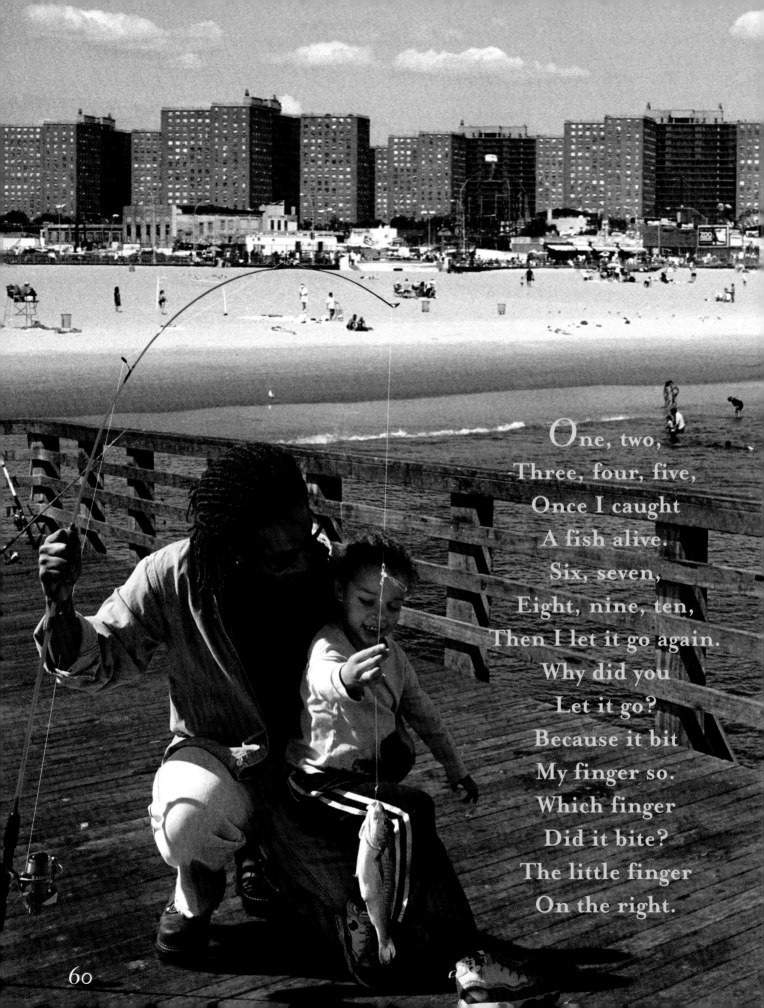

One, two,
Three, four, five,
Once I caught
A fish alive.
Six, seven,
Eight, nine, ten,
Then I let it go again.
Why did you
Let it go?
Because it bit
My finger so.
Which finger
Did it bite?
The little finger
On the right.

Three wise men of Gotham,
They went to sea in a bowl,
And if the bowl had been stronger,
My song had been longer.

# Wee Willie Winkie

Runs through the town,
Upstairs and downstairs,
In his nightgown,
Rapping at the window,
Crying through the lock,
"Are the children all in bed,
For now it's eight o'clock?"

The Neighborhood Mother Goose Copyright © 2004 by
Nina Crews All rights reserved. Manufactured in
China by South China Printing Company Ltd.
www.harperchildrens.com Full-color 35-mm photographs were digitally color-corrected and manipulated
using Adobe Photoshop™ and Adobe Illustrator™. The
text type is Mrs Eaves Bold and Fairfield. Amistad is an
imprint of HarperCollins Publishers, Inc.

LIBRARY OF CONGRESS CATALOGING-IN-PUBLICATION DATA

The Neighborhood Mother Goose / by Nina Crews.
p. cm.
"Greenwillow Books."
Summary: A collection of nursery rhymes, both familiar
and lesser known, illustrated with photographs in a city
setting.
ISBN 0-06-051573-2 (trade). ISBN 0-06-051574-0
(lib. bdg.) 1. Nursery rhymes. [1. Children's poetry.
2. Nursery rhymes.]
I. Crews, Nina, ill. II. Mother Goose. Selections.
PZ8.3.B8245 2004 398.8—dc21 2003041763

10 9
First Edition

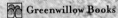 Greenwillow Books

Special thanks to all the
children and adults who modeled
for this book. Ayana Alleyne, Shanise Alleyne,
Austin Carmody, Art Chang, Benjamin Chang,
Amber Charles, Shuquan Isaiah Charles, Maeve Connolly,
Susan Daily, Malcolm Crews, Mariah Crews, Lily Feldman,
Jackson Ferguson, Trager Galinsky, Arielle Griffin, Sofia Heineman,
Diavanna Zarzuela, Olivia Henriques, Josie Hodson, Lucas Hoffner,
Patty Wongpakdee, Marguerite Hughes, Allen Jackson IV, Mary Kornegay,
Mark Littlejohn, Maya Littlejohn, Zita Maria Mahoney, Jonathan Major,
Jack Rader, Todd Rader, Sandra Rivera, JaQuan Shiloh, Callian Stokes,
Alexa Williams, Jonathan Williams, Zachary Williams.


Thanks also to Amy Crews, the Garden of Union Street,
the parents who helped behind the scenes, and my friends
whose advice and support were so valuable.

Mother Goose verses represent a centuries-old oral tradition of rhymes, riddles, jokes, tale telling, and lullabies.
Many rhymes have multiple versions that vary in content or word choice. For this collection, I used THE OXFORD
DICTIONARY OF NURSERY RHYMES, edited by Iona and Peter Opie (Oxford: Oxford University Press, 1997), and
THE ANNOTATED MOTHER GOOSE, arranged and explained by William and Ceil Baring-Gould (New York:
Bramhall House, 1962), as references. When these established sources offered different versions of a rhyme, I selected
the one I felt most suited the book. In some cases, I used wording that I learned as a child and hear used today—after
all, Mother Goose is an oral tradition.